STANDING AT THE HELM

Leadership Development for the Entrepreneur

———————

Dr. Juanita L. Fletcher

STANDING AT THE HELM

ISBN: 978-0692271797

Printed in USA by GHME Productions, Inc.

Scripture quotations taken from biblegateway.com. Material from the Site may be quoted in any form (written, visual, electronic or audio), up to and inclusive of two hundred fifty (250) verses without express written permission of the Zondervan.

Dedication

This book is dedicated to my dad, the late

William S. Thompson.

Thank you for always supporting me in everything that I have ever done. I know that you are still rooting for me in heaven. It is my prayer that I continue to make you proud.

Table of Contents

Table of Contents Cont.

Table of Contents Cont.

Preface

Why did I write a book about leadership? Not just leadership, but leadership specifically targeting leadership for entrepreneurs? There are many books on leadership. While researching this book, I stumbled upon hundreds of books that focus on the development of leaders. On the other hand, finding a book on leadership that contains specific information to guide an entrepreneur was a difficult task, and downright frustrating.

Experience has taught me that leadership skills for an entrepreneur are not necessarily a natural characteristic. In fact, compared to leadership, I have found entrepreneurship to be a much easier task to

STANDING AT THE HELM

accomplish. For one, I can control the amount of effort that will be put forth in my quest for success. However, when it comes to leadership this simply isn't the case. There are a number of traits that entrepreneurs possess which may actually cause an entrepreneur to be a poor leader.

With this thought in mind, the overall goal of this book is to help correct this inherent problem that underlines the success but also is the systematic reason for the failures of most entrepreneurs.

Why does this problem exist?

Well, entrepreneurs generally are self-starters who are able to set a goal and reach that goal without any outside influence or motivation, other than the sense of pride they feel when they have actually reached their goal. Like a mother with her child, an entrepreneur is

bound to their company and therefore requires little coaxing to get the job done. Conversely, employees are not always self-motivated. Unlike the entrepreneur, the employee requires direction, continuous encouragement, and stimulation to accomplish the assigned task. As a result, the entrepreneur must be able to hone in on their leadership skills if they expect to successfully lead their staff.

Entrepreneurs must remember that being an entrepreneur does not automatically qualify one to be a skilled leader. This is a lesson I learned the hard way. Being the oldest of four sisters and the first of twenty-two grandchildren, I had always believed that leadership was a natural part of my DNA. While many of my siblings spent their free time at the park or the playground, at the tender age of nine I started my first business in the kitchen of our family home selling homemade popcorn to the neighborhood children. From there I would go on to create numerous companies, which is why I now consider myself to be a lifetime entrepreneur. Through education, successes, and many, many failures, I now consider myself to be a qualified leader as well.

One thing I have certainly learned is that building a business requires more than one person. It requires an entire team. The owner must be able to properly guide their followers. Without the right leadership it is impossible for a business to succeed. As a result of my own poor leadership skills and my desire to improve, I have created this leadership development guide for entrepreneurs interested in growing a successful business.

As I started to build my company and began to hire my team, I was forced to accept my limitations as a leader. What you are about to read was initially written as an assignment for my doctorate. Through the years, I have updated this book to serve as a guide for entrepreneurs who are interested in improving their leadership skills. Keep in mind, an entrepreneurial leader is only as good as the team they lead.

Finally, I firmly believe that God has provided us a guide for every aspect of life including business ownership. **Proverbs 11:3** tells us *that the integrity of the upright will guide them, but the crookedness of the treacherous will destroy them* (NASB). Even in business there is a standard that the Lord expects us to uphold if we want to remain prosperous. He also lets us know that the hard working will be rewarded. *Do you know a hard-*

working man? He shall be successful and stand before kings! **Proverbs 22:29** (TLB). This book is based on biblical principles and will guide you to becoming a better leader while keeping moral integrity.

I thank God for the vision and determination. I thank my husband James Fletcher whose actions as a leader both in and out of the home have taught me so much. I thank my mother, Priscilla Thompson who calls herself my biggest fan and has supported me from day one. Lastly, I want to thank every professors who has ever mentored, supported or encouraged me. I am so grateful for and proud of this major achievement in my life.

Introduction

Never.

Stop.

Improving.

When standing at the helm, you are the captain of your ship and you are in ultimate command of your vessel. You must be prepared to safely navigate the waters of the sea while simultaneously leading your crew. Your ability to effectively lead your crew could possibly be the difference between life and death in many cases. In business you will find many similarities between weathering the storms of the sea and the struggles of your company. This book provides important lessons necessary for one to improve their leadership skills and essentially grow their business.

I can personally attest to the lessons I have learned as I put this book together. So many areas that I thought I had reached a point of achievement, I was shown my flaws and where I needed to improve. As an entrepreneur I want to be successful. To be successful, I need help. I need a team who believes in my vision and is willing to work to help me achieve it. This book provides guidance for any entrepreneur interested in growing their business through effective leadership.

But Ruth replied, "Don't ask me to leave you and turn back. Wherever you go, I will go; wherever you live, I will live. Your people will be my people, and your God will be my God." – **Ruth 1:16** *(NLT)*

Ruth said this to Naomi as a show of faith and loyalty. As a leader it is your responsibility to procure your team. Your job is not to only give direction but to nurture, support, and bring the very best out of them. When done right, a leader's most prized possession is the loyalty of their team. This is something that is not only a challenge to obtain but a challenge to maintain as well. *Standing at the Helm* provides readers a closer look at what it takes to acquire and lead a loyal team successfully by targeting three key elements of leadership vital for entrepreneurial success: strategic thinking, structure and style, and global thinking. Since this book is based on Christian principles, biblical instruction and reflection is included at the end of every segment.

Part 1

Become the kind of leader that people would follow voluntarily; even if you had no title or position.

— Brian Tracy

STANDING AT THE HELM

Leadership

No matter the industry, entrepreneurship is risky business. According to the Small Business Association, 50% of all new business operations never survive long enough to see their fifth year. While there are numerous reasons why companies fail, one leading cause of failure is poor leadership. Because of this, entrepreneurs must work to become more effective leaders in their chosen field. The first step for the entrepreneur is to gain some understanding of leadership.

Leadership is an important aspect that every entrepreneur must understand and appreciate. In essence, leadership refers to the process by which an individual uses their influence to steer a group of people towards accomplishing a common objective (Northouse, 2007). Leadership is a combination of unique traits and personalities possessed by certain individuals, which enable such individuals to influence others towards achieving certain goals (ibid.).

Please make note: there is a difference between entrepreneurial leadership and more traditional forms of leadership. Entrepreneurial leadership is quite different from other leadership styles, in that it is pragmatic in nature and is centered on creating value in an industry, along with solving problems. However, it is still similar in that it evokes astonishing effort (Surie & Ashley, 2008).

Entrepreneurial leadership is geared towards value creation for all stakeholders of the enterprise through combining a unique innovation with other resources and

services in response to an identified opportunity (Darling, Keefe, & Ross, 2007).

Years ago I was the owner of a property and casualty insurance agency. As an agent I was free to operate my company individually as long as I was able to successfully manage my clientele. When I decided I was ready to expand my company and open a second location in a neighboring city, I was forced to bring in additional agents. This move taught me the importance of leadership skills. As an entrepreneur working alone, I could control the amount effort put forth for every task. Once I began to bring in staff, suddenly I had to motivate others to not only do their job but to do it well. I didn't know how to duplicate myself in my team, which is the job of every leader.

As a result of my inexperience as a leader, I was unable to properly lead the team that I needed to successfully expand my company. I struggled to make it work for six months before being forced to make the painful decision to close my second location. This was a major lesson for me.

Chapter 1

Trust

Despite the different types of leadership, there are certain core characteristics common to all successful leaders. First is the ability to be trusted. Trust is at the heart of all leader/follower relationships. Trust delivers results: people follow, achieve, and stay with leaders they trust (Shelton, 2010). When leaders are found to be untrustworthy even once, employee moral will decrease, they become less engaged and are less likely to follow the vision set before them by their leader from there on out (Simmons, 2002). When seeking to develop meaningful leader/follower relationships, all leaders must first establish trust.

Titus 2:7 discusses leadership: *"Show yourself in all respects to be a model of good works, and in your teaching show integrity, dignity,"* (ESV).

If you are trustworthy and blameless in your actions, even those who are dead set against you may eventually be turned around. Without trust it is impossible to lead successfully. I can recall how I felt the first time I had someone in leadership lie to me. It changed my view of the leader and ultimately my view of the organization. The dynamics between he and I were changed forever. Where I was once willing to work well past what was required of me, I found myself only willing to do what was required. This happens all too often. Therefore, if your aim is to lead successfully, developing trust must be at the top of your list. To be considered a trustworthy leader, there are four essential characteristics you must possess: authenticity, integrity, a system of values, and the ability to inspire.

Chapter 2

Authenticity

An authentic leader is a consistent leader. Not only do authentic leaders possess a true desire to relentlessly live by their values, they also lead from their hearts and with their minds, and have an established passion for their main goal (George, Sims, McLean, & Mayer, 2007). Followers are less likely to believe in the leadership of someone who is less than sincere. As the leader of your company you play an extremely important role in the development of your team. Your employees watch everything you do. The behavior of leaders directly affects that of their subordinates, a fact that many leaders fail to realize or admit (Dwyer, 2007).

Moreover, they are self-disciplined and believe in their own worth. Opposed to amassing power, prestige, and money for their own gain, authentic leaders' main interest is in empowering their subordinates to be the flag bearers of change. Their leadership is a service to their followers. As much as they are guided by the mind, they also uphold virtues of the heart: compassion and passion (George, 2007).

For the entrepreneurial leader, it is vital to be authentic because much of your success depends heavily on your constituents. To be authentic, God gives instruction in **Romans 12:2**: *"Do not allow this world to mold you in its own image. Instead, be transformed from the inside out by renewing your mind. As a result, you will be able to discern what God wills and whatever God finds good, pleasing, and complete,"* (VOICE).

I have had the displeasure of working under leaders who clearly acted one way in front of the boss and another when we were together as a team. A prime example of this would be a supervisor who requires everyone to work extra hard just before an inspection by the owners, yet day-to-day operations are permitted to fall below company standards. This is the act of a double-minded person. As **James 1:8** states: *A double minded man is unstable in all his ways* (KJV). No one wants to follow a leader who is inconsistent in their leadership. A double-minded leader is considered to be unreliable and untrustworthy. Since the authenticity of business leaders has a lasting effect on the mindset of their followers and can hinder a leader's ability to motivate, it is vital for entrepreneurs to remain authentic.

STANDING AT THE HELM

Chapter 3

Integrity

Next on the list is integrity. Integrity is a crucial trait for all leaders who wish to have influence amongst their followers. Until leaders are able to establish an image of competence and trust in the minds of subordinates, they will find it extremely difficult to guide their team (Gray & Densten, 2007). Integrity and being trustworthy are the biggest desires of leaders in respect to entrepreneurial leadership (Darling, Keefe, & Ross, 2007). Integrity comes from within a person; it is a quality that assures the subordinates that what they see, hear, or read can be relied on without having to be qualified.

An entrepreneurial leader with integrity influences their employees in such a way that they can be relied on to facilitate accomplishment of operational excellence in the organization (ibid.). Integrity can also help entrepreneurs with employee retention, loyalty, and commitment. Per Kouzes and Posner (2007), most employees are unwilling to entrust a leader with their career and security if the leader does not practice what they preach.

To be a leader with integrity is not always easy for the entrepreneur. The temptation to do wrong is great every single day. As an entrepreneur, you are in business to make money, and, hopefully lots of it. In our quest for money, sometimes greed does set in; but in most cases an entrepreneur might decide to cut corners simply because they are trying to survive. **Proverbs 28:6** reads: *It is*

better to be a pauper walking in integrity than a

dishonest man, even if he is rich (VOICE). When I first

started my insurance agency, I spent the first six months

of business wondering if God even remembered my

name. Business was not slow, business was completely

dead. I was selling less than ten policies a month. I was

the feeling the pressure of overdue rent and a dwindling

savings account.

One day, I had an elderly gentleman come in and

ask to take out an insurance policy. This customer drove a

cab for a living and he kept his earnings from the day in a

brown paper bag. I gave the customer my best quote,

which he happily accepted. Instead of counting out the

deposit amount, he handed me the entire bag and walked

away. Minutes after meeting me he was trusting me to

STANDING AT THE HELM

count out the correct amount and give the remainder back to him.

As I emptied the bag of crumpled ones, tens, and twenties, the list of bills kept running through my mind. At that moment I had to make a decision. If I took a little extra for myself it really wouldn't make much of a difference to him, since he didn't know how much he had in the first place. Here is where integrity comes into play. As the leader of the company, leadership sets the example that the employees will follow. If leadership lacks integrity all trust will be lost.

I made the decision to remain a leader with integrity. I gathered his crumpled money, placed it back into the brown bag and handed his money to him.

36 | P a g e

Chapter 4

Values

The third leadership characteristic to be discussed is values. A leader must also have values. Values refer to common rules and beliefs that regulate employee behavior and attitudes, making a certain manner of conduct less acceptable than others, personally and socially (Jones, Jimmieson, & Griffiths, 2005). Though integration of ethics with efficiency is often possible for the majority of successful entrepreneurial leaders, entrepreneurial leaders are often seen as ignorant to values and ethics in their unwavering pursuit of corporate goals and success (Surie & Ashley, 2008). Business owners should keep in mind that because they are easily identifiable, their actions are watched continuously by their employees (Kuratko, 2007). To create a "values-driven" organization, leaders must exhibit the characteristics they wish their subordinates to remember (Dickson, Smith, Grojean, & Ehrhart, 2001).

When you are placed in a leadership position you are constantly forced to question your ethical position. Even more so when you are an entrepreneur, because you don't have the accountability that a hired leader would have. As an entrepreneur, it is your responsibility to put rules, procedures, and guidelines in place for your company. The guidelines that you put in place cannot be for certain employees or customers and not for others. As the owner of the company, the leader's actions will either validate or cancel out these rules. Take, for example, an issue I had with a customer who was also a friend. This

customer/friend allowed her policy to cancel for nonpayment three days prior to a major accident for which she was at fault. Based on our friendship she asked if I would be willing to accept her payment and backdate her insurance policy so that the medical bills of the other driver would be covered. Now this was a real dilemma.

I had a duty to the insurance company that I represented to uphold the rules of the policy as well as to the staff that I was responsible to train. If a leader's actions do not align with their words, if there is any ambiguity in the system of ethics established for the company, followers will view the leader as a fraud, and thus leadership will lose all believability (Malphurs, 2004). I made the decision to stand firm in my beliefs and refused to back date her policy. As a leader, your actions will either confirm or disprove you to be a trustworthy. As **Proverbs 20:11** confirms: *Even children show what they are by what they do; you can tell if they are honest and good"* (GNT). Therefore, it is important that a leader remains ethical and upholds the values of the company at all times. To do otherwise will cost the leader greatly.

Chapter 5

Inspiration

The final characteristic is the ability to inspire. Leaders have the ability to inspire through shared vision. A leader's shared vision is a strong tactical device for inspiring followers (Dwivedi, 2006). Entrepreneurial leaders who are able to inspire their team will find that employees are more willing to work hard for them. Therefore, it is essential for leaders to ensure their subjects are constantly inspired and motivated (Ellis, 2004). To become an inspiring leader, entrepreneurs must strive to be passionate, be honest about their weaknesses, genuinely care about people, share their vision, become storytellers, go beyond the expected, and be responsible but not accountable for everything

(Wager, 2011).

When inspiring your team through storytelling,

you are basically selling them the idea of how things

could be. I suspect this is what Steve Jobs did when he

returned to Apple and turned the company around in

1996 or how GM CEO, Ed Whitacre was able to get the

company behind him to turn GM around after its

bankruptcy and government bailout. As an

entrepreneurial leader, we have to learn how to inspire

our team. We have to sell our vision to them and

encourage them to see where we are trying to go. After

all, it is our team that will ultimately get us to the next

level and help to make our company a success.

Have you have ever patronized a business where

the employees where clearly uninspired? How was the

customer service? How anxious were you to return to that business? As an entrepreneur, you must keep your staff in the loop of the company. They must feel like their contributions are valued and that they are appreciated. An inspired employee will always go beyond what is asked.

STANDING AT THE HELM

God's Instruction

FOR THE OVERSEER MUST BE BLAMELESS, AS GOD'S STEWARD; NOT SELF-PLEASING, NOT EASILY ANGERED, NOT GIVEN TO WINE, NOT VIOLENT, NOT GREEDY FOR DISHONEST GAIN; BUT GIVEN TO HOSPITALITY, A LOVER OF GOOD, SOBER MINDED, FAIR, HOLY, SELF-CONTROLLED. **TITUS 1:7-8** (WEB)

To be a leader, you must be respected as such. No one will respect a leader who is only interested in self. When a leader is found to be dishonest and untrustworthy, that leader is deemed incapable of inspiring his team or growing their organization.

Is your leadership trustworthy?

Rate your leadership now:

Never (N) 1 2 3 4 5 6 7 8 Always (A)

_____ Do you always lead by example?

_____ Do you practice your values consistently?

_____ Are you willing to lose money for your values?

_____ Do you also adhere to the rules you have created?

_____ Do your team consider you to be inspirational?

What have you gleaned?_____

_____

_____

_____

_____

_____

_____

_____

_____

_____

_____

_____

_____

_____

_____

_____

Part 2

"*Leaders establish the vision for the future and set the strategy for getting there; they cause change. They motivate and inspire others to go in the right direction and they, along with everyone else, sacrifice to get there.*"

– John Kotter

Think Strategically

Once they understand the definition of leadership and the basic characteristics of a trustworthy leader, entrepreneurs should seek an understanding of four key elements of entrepreneurial leadership: strategic thinking, organizational structure, leadership style, and global outreach. In business, strategic thinkers endeavor to create value, promote innovation through risk taking, invent new substitutes, exploit their strengths, tactically shape the future, explore finding superior substitutes, and unequivocally commit to achieving practical results (Wing, 1997).

The thought pattern of a strategic thinker is very similar to that of a racecar driver. A racecar driver is a multifaceted thinker. While keeping his eyes on the road, the driver also considers the condition of the tires, the brakes, the track surface, the distance of competitors, and his ability to communicate effectively with members of his team. Simultaneously, the driver remains a quick thinker in the midst of extreme pressures.

To survive, entrepreneurial leaders must be able to think strategically. Strategic thinking is different from day-to-day thinking. Strategic thinking is a strategic problem-solving method that merges creative and differing mindsets with a realistic yet convergent approach (Bonn, 2005). In addition to envisaging a possible future full of positive changes, strategic thinking seeks to develop, new, innovative approaches to finding a leading edge in this competitive world (Casey, 2010). Thinking strategically is biblical, as we learn in

Proverbs 14:15, which reads: *The simple believes everything, but the prudent gives thought to his steps* (ESV). A successful leader understands the importance of thinking through each move. In other words, think strategically.

Chapter 6

Innovation

I can remember a time when using your imagination was encouraged. As a child you played with an empty box pretending that it was an enchanted castle. You used your imagination to create all kinds of games. In today's economy being creative is a requirement. Leaders who think strategically exhibit specific thinking skills, such as the ability to encourage and promote novelty and innovation. Innovation is defined as value addition through change. Narvekar and Jain (2010) define innovation as the process undertaken to transform an original idea into a quantifiable business value for an enterprise (Ljepava, 2010). Moreover, experts state that businesses build and sustain a competitive edge through innovation (Transport Industries Benefit, 2009).

The 21st century has been described as "the century of innovation…" where the competitive edge of companies as well as countries will be characterized by innovation (Barrett, 2010). Finally, the key to succeeding in business lies in the capability to carry out problem-solving tasks, both ingeniously and innovatively (Saloner, 2011).

As the leader of an organization, you are expected to be able to think creatively and innovatively. Leaders who are creative also create others who are creative, although it is important to note that leadership does not automatically guarantee creativity. However, creativity can be taught, learned, substantiated, and is critical in the human development process (Balkin, 1990). Leaders

must not only take the time to grow creatively, but also to encourage followers to be creative as well. After all, the leader cannot succeed alone.

Strategic thinkers create an environment that is conducive to generating greater creativity, are supportive of the creative efforts of subordinates, and regularly embrace opportunities to think outside the norm of everyday operations. Creativity is a core trait for strategic thinkers; they must explore to discover new approaches as well as come up will more efficient ways of doing things (Bonn, 2005). Most entrepreneurial leaders understand the importance of creativity. Creativity and innovation is absolutely vital to any company's ability to maintain and build a competitive advantage.

It has been proven that a lack of creativity will ultimately lead to failure. We all can name a number of major business chains that have gone out of business over the last ten years as a result of their inability to innovate. Entrepreneurial leaders who wish to avoid this same fate must improve their ability to innovate and create. Last note: creating new solutions and ideas so as to gain competitive advantage is the key purpose of strategy (Bonn, 2005).

There are many different ways to think creatively. My process always starts and finishes with seeking God. When I started my last business, I prayed and asked God to give me an idea that was new and different. I found myself listing not only my own gifts, talents and hobbies, but that of my two daughters. After six months of tweaking and rewriting I came up with an idea for a girl's party center. What made my idea different was the fact that it incorporated the ideas and talents of my entire

family. As a singer, there was a process that I went through before I could release a project to the public. So, I thought to myself, why not make the process a novelty so that everyone could experience the feeling of being a singing diva. For two to three hours girls could get makeovers, a professional photo shoot and even record in a real recording studio. Nothing like this had ever been done before. The idea was new and creative. The major point I am trying to make, is that creativity can come from anywhere. There is no price minimum, age limitation or level of education requirement for creativity. In other words, anyone can be creative. An entrepreneurial leader who thinks strategically recognizes the benefits of creativity and will use it to gain a competitive edge.

Chapter 7

Flexibility

Strategic thinkers also understand the importance of flexibility. The ability to change direction and switch gears is vital in this technological age. The intricacies of modern business require leaders to use new work methods; therefore, flexibility is an extremely necessary skill. Successful leaders that are seen as full of potential may be deemed unfit to lead and thus sacked, demoted, or held stagnant in their career if they are incapable of adapting to change (Calarco & Gurvis, 2006).

The entrepreneurial leader without the ability to adapt is guaranteed to experience business closure eventually. For the small business entrepreneur, change is a daily requirement. Nothing is ever written in stone. Entrepreneurial leaders who cannot change cannot compete and will not survive.

So many entrepreneurs have watched their businesses die because they refused to change with the times. Some entrepreneurs are unable to release an idea once its time has clearly passed. **Ecclesiastes 3:1** tells us *there is a time for everything, and everything on earth has its special season* (NCV). As an entrepreneur, you can never marry an idea. You simply cannot afford to. Entrepreneurial leaders should always remain flexible and must create an organizational environment which is able to adapt and transition as needed.

To become more flexible, leaders should begin to view change as another opportunity to learn something

new. Here are three flexibility skills every entrepreneurial leader should work on developing:

- Cognitive flexibility: the ability to use a variety of thinking strategies and mental frameworks.

- Emotional flexibility: the ability to vary one's approach to dealing with one's own emotions and those of others.

- Dispositional flexibility (or personality-based flexibility): the ability to remain optimistic and at the same time realistic (Calarco & Gurvis, 2006).

When I first opened my party center I had the idea that I would create a party for women to come and enjoy the facility as well. We were already servicing their children, so in my mind it was only natural to provide a service for the parent as well. However, I soon learned that there simply wasn't a market for this service. It was also not cost effective to provide parties for adults. I pursued the adult customer for about three months before deciding to cancel this service. All too often entrepreneurs decide that something is a good idea and refuse to listen to their customers. It is imperative to avoid marrying your ideas. In your quest for entrepreneurial leadership success always remain flexible in all endeavors. Don't allow your inability to change kill your dreams.

Chapter 8

Vision

Another important element of strategic thinking is vision casting. Vision is defined as a well-developed idea (Carland & Carland Jr., 2012). People are most creative and contributory in ways that fully exploit their skills and talents in the presence of vision, as it gives focus and inspires imagination (Bonn, 2005). A vision that is shared throughout the organization fosters commitment rather than compliance and creates a sense of commonality that permeates the whole organization (Collins & Porras, 1998). A vision is used to present and communicate the goals and objective of entrepreneurial leadership. It provides a reference point around which information is absorbed by entrepreneurial leadership (Majumdar, 2008).

Since business ventures are little more than the manifestation of the entrepreneur's vision, creating and instilling the leader's vision is the most crucial aspect of entrepreneurial leadership (Carland & Carland Jr., 2012). An entrepreneur who successfully casts vision into the organization will notice improved employee morale, a deeper sense of commitment, and a more cohesive team effort amongst subordinates. Please note, no vision exists if followers are not able to visualize the vision; therefore, the leader must be able develop a mental image of the firm's goals and aspirations (Miller, 1995).

As an entrepreneur and leader of my business, I have found my most vital strategic tool to be company vision. When delineating the basis of a system, it is very

crucial to have a vision. It represents a postulated future image of to where the investor wants to drive their product or service in the subject marked. Moreover, vision also plays the role of attracting, encouraging, and motivating the staff in the enterprise (Majumdar, 2008). Since vision is used to present and communicate the goals and objectives of entrepreneurial leadership, the set core values are thus reinforced. For any venture to be successful, it is important to have a clear vision (Majumdar, 2008). In my business, I have worked hard to make sure that my team all have a clear understanding of the vision that I have for the company.

A leader's shared vision is a strong tactical device for encouraging followers (Dwivedi, 2006); however, all leaders must understand how to best communicate that vision to the follower. If passion is portrayed by a leader, their subordinates can bring the needed change in the organization, showing their hope for the future (Mancheno-Smoak, Endres, Polak, & Athanasaw, 2009). With this thought in mind, exactly how does a leader communicate through passion? A leader should give a clear picture of their vision and the possible outcome of that vision if the leader desires followers to take part (Stanley, 2009). Stanley advises leaders to illustrate their intended destination using a clear verbal depiction (Stanley, 1999). God left instruction in **Habakkuk 2:2**, which reads: *Write down the vision; write it clearly on clay tablets so whoever reads it can run to tell others* (NCV). My company definitely has been built around my personal vision of what I believe God has told me my business will one day be.

Chapter 9

Future-Orientation

Strategic thinkers are also future-oriented and utilize their long-term perspective. This is a skill that enables leaders to make decisions today that will position the company for success tomorrow. Additionally, this skill will give leaders an appreciation and understanding of value investments for the future (Buhler, 2005). Strategic thinkers are mainly focused on set goals. Their actions are carried out with the future in mind. The driving force is the future and thus most of their actions are geared towards creating a successful future in their niche (Thoms, 2004).

Strategic intent drives strategic leaders to look into and plan for an uncertain future far beyond the present. Strategic intent is when the intended goal or objective is clearly set but the means of achieving it are not so well known (Quong & Walker, 2010). Leaders who are future thinkers are also comfortable with planning, tend to be good at creating a vision, and usually have detailed cognitive images of what the future can be (ibid.). These are critical skills for the entrepreneurial leader. One must be able to anticipate future buying trends of the consumer and be able to make future plans to meet the needs of tomorrow. Much of your time will be spent trying to stay ahead of trends, fads, changes in your market, competition, economic issues that may affect your business, changes in technology, and the list continues. Therefore, improving future thinking skills is

highly necessary. As a small business owner, you must pay attention to trends that could impact your business, for the positive or the negative.

I can remember when beeper businesses were the big thing for entrepreneurs. Pagers were very popular and since these types of businesses were fairly cheap to start many, many entrepreneurs happily embraced the beeper business. Now... how many pager companies do you know of today? This type of business disappeared about as fast as it was introduced. While larger companies had the finances to change their inventory to match the changing times, entrepreneurs were not so lucky. Entrepreneurial leaders must always pay attention to what and how trends will affect their business.

Chapter 10

Balance

Lastly, strategic thinkers understand the importance of work, rest, and balance; yet, many entrepreneurial leaders fail in the area of self-care because they are either unable or unwilling to recognize the limitations of the human body. All too often, entrepreneurial leaders are apt to wear their exhaustion like a badge of honor, even though it's been proven that people accomplish so much more when they are adequately rested (Maitland, 2010). There is a well-recognized relationship between overworking and health-related issues. In comparison to people who work seven hours a day, people who often work ten to eleven hours a day have a higher risk of getting critical heart diseases, such as cardiac arrest (Maitland, 2010).

Leaders must realize that working to this degree simply does not benefit the company. People are only able to share what they have (Black, 2013). God knew the importance of being rested, which is why He left instruction in **Leviticus 23:3**, which reads:

> *You have six days in which to do your work, but remember that the seventh day, the Sabbath, is a day of rest. On that day do not work, but gather for worship. The Sabbath belongs to the LORD, no matter where you live. (GNT)*

Leaders should regularly rejuvenate their body, mind, spirit, and emotions so as to have the needed energy to carry out daily tasks (Milazzo, 2012). We need to listen to our bodies and take the time necessary to rejuvenate. It is essential that entrepreneurial leaders

manage the physical and emotional strain that comes with growing a business by making rest and rejuvenation a priority every week (Klein, 2006).

Everyone, even talented and brilliant people, has a cognitive limit that once reached, the performance of the individuals is affected (Moyer, 2006). All leader must learn the value of making rest a priority.

Entrepreneurs! Stop wearing exhaustion as a badge of honor. You are no good to your business, your family, or yourself if you work your body to the point of exhaustion.

God's Instruction

A Strong Man Knows How To Use His Strength, But A Person With Knowledge Is Even More Powerful. After All, With The Right Strategy You Can Wage War, And With Many Advisers There Is Victory. **Proverbs 24: 5-6** (Gw)

To have a successful business, an entrepreneurial leader must always think strategically. Take the time to consider your strategy in all endeavors.

Are you a strategic thinking leader?

Rate your leadership now:

Never (N) 1 2 3 4 5 6 7 8 Always (A)

_____ Do you consistently seek new ideas for your business?

_____ Do you view change as an opportunity to learn something new?

_____ Do you share your vision for the future of your company with your employees?

_____ Do you mentally invest in the future of your company?

_____ Do your seek balance in your life?

What have you gleaned?_____

_____

_____

_____

_____

_____

_____

_____

_____

_____

_____

_____

_____

_____

_____

Part 3

"The neglected leadership role is the designer of the ship"

– Peter Senge

Organizational Structure

There are three key elements in the definition of organizational structure. Organizational structure entails official reporting relationships, including the number of levels in the hierarchy and the managers' and supervisors' spheres of control. Additionally, this structure categorizes the grouping together of individuals and departments into the total organization. Lastly, organizational structure encompasses the design of systems to ensure effective communication, coordination, and integration of efforts across departments (Daft, 2007). An example of the first organizational structure can be found in 1

Corinthians 12:28 where God designed the structure of the church.

As stated by Lincoln and Kalleberg (1990) in Lambert, Hogan, and Allen (2006), various dimensional structures are employed in organizations to achieve influence, management, and control over employees. Organizational structure is vital for the entrepreneurial leader, because in most situations it is the entrepreneur who will actually choose the structure of their business, whether it be intentional or unintentional.

Business leaders must be aware of different organizational structures if they are to select the structure that best fits their business model. For this purpose, five organizational structures are listed: centralized, decentralized, shamrock, matrix, and boundaryless.

Chapter 11

Centralization

One of these organizational structures is centralization. Centralization is defined as the structure of management where the top management levels make all the key decisions regarding the organization (Seeds & Khade, 2008). The centralized organizational structure tightly regulates the amount of control bestowed on employees to make decisions critical to both their jobs (that is, autonomy/job autonomy) and the organization (that is, participation in decision-making) (Lambert, Hogan, & Allen, 2006). Entrepreneurial leaders who delegate little or no authority to subordinates are operating under a centralized organizational structure.

Under this structure, the entrepreneurial leader takes steps to retain power at the top level of the organizational hierarchy (Nordmeyer, 2013). Under this organizational structure, entrepreneurs with a centralized leadership approach are easily motivated, organized, and goal-oriented, given that communication flows from top-down to the staff. In very competitive environments that are characterized by fast-paced, high-stake, and time-critical emergencies a centralized leadership strategy plays a big part in succeeding (Fraher, A., 2010). Control is another benefit of operating under this structure for the business owner; however, on the negative side, this organizational structure does not support innovation and is heavily dependent upon its leader.

Entrepreneurial leaders of small companies generally operate under the centralized structure out of

sheer necessity, although it is not uncommon for a large company to use this structure as well. For the small business, an entrepreneurial leader may only have one or two employees. As a result, the leader may initially have no choice in their business structure; however, entrepreneurial leaders should avoid locking themselves into any one structure. Allow for flexibility as your company grows. When I first opened my company, I started out without any employees; therefore, the organizational structure which best fit my company at that time was centralized. However, as my company began to grow in location and product, the centralized structure was no longer a good fit.

This is not to say that large firms do not utilize centralized organizational structures. Apple is a great example of a large company that utilizes this structure.

This structure works well because, while the company itself is large, the product line is not. While the company is certainly innovative, the company focuses more attention on improving its current products, which allows the company to thrive under this organizational structure.

Chapter 12

Decentralization

Decentralization is the opposing organizational structure. Schilling describes decentralization as being concerned with the degree to which decision-making authority is pushed down to lower levels of the firm (Seeds & Khade, 2008). In a decentralized organizational structure, the leader delegates considerable control and responsibilities to the employees, especially in small-scale business establishments (Nordmeyer, 2013).

A decentralized leadership strategy creates a good environment for the free-flow of ideas. The less hierarchical structure is best suited for an organization that thrives on creative solutions and innovation from skilled and talented individuals who have a clear understanding of the role they play in the organization as well as the business environment (Fraher, 2010). In a decentralized structure, entrepreneurs must be able to train other leaders. It is the job of the leader to duplicate themselves by equipping followers with the necessary skills of leadership. In this organizational structure, the level of excellence will depend upon the leader's ability to instill leadership skills within their subordinates. For a small- to medium-sized company, a decentralized organizational structure would work well since this structure is designed to delegate responsibilities to top management to middle- and lower-level mangers within the organization. Delegating responsibility will essentially free up the leader and allow ownership to focus their attention more on major decisions.

PepsiCo is a great example of a decentralized company. PepsiCo has three branches: PepsiCo Americas Foods, PepsiCo Americas Beverages, and PepsiCo International. All three units operate under a decentralized organizational structure, with operational decisions made within the separate business units. The individual units are governed by corporate policies.

Chapter 13

Shamrock

The "shamrock" organization is defined as an organizational structure with three branches or tiers in which people can be employed and organizations can be linked. The three groups are professional managers, contracted specialists, such as advertising, computing, or catering personnel, and a flexible labor force discharging part-time, temporary, or seasonal roles (Daft, 2007). The shamrock is fitting for medium to large firms; however, this structure can be incorporated in smaller firms if structured correctly. In an entrepreneurial leadership situation, this structure has several key points. First, followers are divided into three sections. Secondly, under the shamrock, the leader's influence may be limited because of the structure itself. The contracted specialists are not followers.

I am waiting for my company to grow into this structure. As the founder and editor-in-chief of ACHI Magazine, I am tasked with the duty of developing the company's organizational structure. Currently we only have two divisions; however, we will soon be divided into three different areas. This structure may present a challenge for some small business owners; however, the benefits far outweigh the challenges.

Chapter 14

Matrix

The next organizational design to be discussed is the "matrix." This organizational structure was created with the intent of joining the productivity of functional design with the flexibility and responsiveness of the matrix form. The makeup of the matrix organization generally encompasses twofold command duties and can be assigned to functional departments (e.g. marketing, production, and engineering) and to product or marketing departments. The former are oriented to specialized in-house resources while the latter focus on outputs (Davis & Lawrence, 1978).

To understand, we should try to visualize the matrix organization as two structures, each with an individual set of responsibilities and a different group of leaders. Leaders on the functional side of the matrix are responsible for assigning experts to projects, helping them maintain their skills and acquire new ones, as well as monitoring their execution with respect to the standards of their functional specialty (Hatch & Cunliffe, 2006).

There are several different industries which operate under the matrix organizational structure, such as shipyards, construction, and even aviation industries. Any company that can be divided into two parts can use this structure. In an entrepreneurial situation, a business can be divided between sales and administration or business and production. The company that I currently

own operates under this organizational structure. As the owner of a magazine, my company also has two different departments: sales and production.

Chapter 15

Boundaryless

The final organizational structure to be reviewed is the "boundaryless" structure. The "boundaryless" structure is a lot similar to living organisms. Just like cell membranes in living organisms, its borders (in all dimensions: external, horizontal, vertical, and geographic) are strong enough to give shape and at the same time permeable enough for effortless flow of ideas as well as information throughout the organization. It has a shape that is neither fixed nor static. As time goes, changes may be implemented regarding horizontal boundaries to join departments in new ways while vertical boundaries may shrink to only having a few management levels (Ashkenas, 1999).

The "boundaryless" organization is perfect for the ever-growing global economy, and entrepreneurs are flocking to this organizational structure in droves. However, entrepreneurs should be forewarned that the "boundaryless" structure presents a whole new set of leadership challenges. Much of the task of leadership will be accomplished by way of telecommunication and virtual technologies. Therefore, entrepreneurial leaders must prepare themselves to lead remotely.

Today the "boundaryless" organizational structure is quite popular. Numerous well-known companies function under this structure such as General Electric, Ikea, Saturn and Walmart/Proctor & Gamble, just to name a few. This structure is even popular amongst

government agencies, such as Centers for Medicare & Medicaid Services, NASA, and USDA. This structure is widely popular because of the fast paced, global world that we live in today. Under the "boundaryless" structure, decisions are made by the leaders who are closest to the issue and therefore will have to live with the consequences of their decision (Ashkenas, 1999).

God's Instruction

So I TOOK THE HEADS OF YOUR TRIBES, WISE MEN,

AND KNOWN, AND MADE THEM HEADS OVER YOU,

CAPTAINS OF THOUSANDS, AND CAPTAINS OF

HUNDREDS, AND CAPTAINS OF FIFTIES, AND CAPTAINS

OF TENS, AND OFFICERS, ACCORDING TO YOUR TRIBES.

DEUTERONOMY 1:15 (WEB)

A thriving business can sometimes feel like both a blessing and a curse. To suddenly be inundated with a large influx of customers or clients without an organizational structure in place can be quite overwhelming. Make sure that your structure happens on purpose and not by chance.

Are you the lead designer of your ship?

Rate your leadership now:

Never (N) 1 2 3 4 5 6 7 8 Always (A)

_____ Do you enforce the organizational structure of your business?

_____ Do you clarify your organizational structure to your employees?

_____ Does your leadership style match your organizational structure?

_____ Do you recognize your organizational structure in your day-to-day operations?

What have you gleaned? _____

_____

_____

_____

_____

_____

_____

_____

_____

_____

_____

_____

_____

_____

_____

_____

_____

Part 4

"Styles are tailor made to different situations. Different leaders must have their own styles and these styles must be able to adapt to different people and situations."

— John Ng

Leadership Style

Entrepreneurs cannot think of organizational structure without considering leadership style. Manfred Kets de Vries defines leadership style as the point of interaction between three things: the leader's character type, the followers' character types, and the situation (Kippenberger, 2002).

Leadership style calls attention to the actions of the leader, and centers completely on what the leader does and how the leader acts, including the manner in which the leader acts toward followers in different circumstances (Northouse, 2007).

Leadership styles are either task-motivated or relationship-motivated. Task-motivated leadership styles are focused mainly on reaching a goal; conversely, relationship-motivated leaders are concerned with developing close interpersonal relationships (Northouse, 2007).

For the task-motivated leader, the principal need is to get the job done, while the need to satisfy personal matters is secondary. However, the relationship-motivated leader will view their least-favored colleague in more positive terms because their primary need is to get along with people. Completing a task is less important for the relationship-motivated entrepreneur (ibid.).

When determining the style of leadership, entrepreneurs should keep in mind that there is no perfect leadership style. Different circumstances and relationships, as well as the capabilities of the leader along with those of his subordinates determine the most

suitable leadership style (Gatto, 1992). Entrepreneurial leaders should allow the situation to determine the appropriate style of leadership.

It is common practice for good leaders to instinctively switch between leadership styles, depending upon the needs of the team that they are leading and the task at hand (Mindtools.com). Conversely, less experienced leaders who are unaware of the various leadership models will usually gravitate to a leadership style that feels most comfortable. As an entrepreneurial leader, business owners should become familiar with the various leadership styles to better lead their staff.

Chapter 16

Transactional

An example of the task-oriented leadership style is the transactional leader. The transactional leadership style awards a reward or punishes the subordinate subject to his level of performance and contingent reinforcement, whether positive or negative Contingent Reward (CR), or passive management-by-exception and active management-by-exception (Bass, 1998). Compliance of the subordinates is core in transactional leadership (Giri & Santra, 2010).

Additionally, the personal needs or personal development of the subordinates are not areas of focus for the transactional leader. The subordinates are rewarded with valuable things as a way of motivating them towards both the organizational agendas as well as those of the subordinates (Northouse, 2007).

Entrepreneurial leaders are often transactional. The entrepreneurial leadership style is pragmatic in nature and is centered on creating value in an industry along with solving problems (Surie & Ashley, 2008). As an entrepreneur, a leader is naturally motivated by goals and achievements. While this leadership style may not always be the best, it is the most common. Large companies with little need for creativity operate well under this leadership style. Manufacturing and industrial companies with assembly line type production fair well under the transactional leader. These leaders view success as the completion of an assigned task.

This leadership style does not provide the best results for small businesses where the leadership greatly depends upon the team. Employees need to feel like more than a number. The transactional leadership style focuses on the task rather than the person.

Chapter 17

Values-Based

Values-based leadership is an example of relationship-oriented leadership. This leadership style encourages employee loyalty and retention. The mission and vision of an organization with a values-based leadership style are developed from superordinate values (Surie & Ashley, 2008). Furthermore, the actions of leaders reinforces the mission and conveys great expectations on the part of the staff by expressing confidence in their capacity to deliver as expected (ibid.).

A values-based leader encourages, listens, understands the needs of their staff, and subsequently influences them to instigate the needed changes towards achieving the shared vision. Values-based leadership entails addressing employee needs and wants by way of assisting them appreciate and work towards the shared vision of the company (Rakov, 2001).

God has given biblical instruction for the values-based leader in **1 Peter 5:2-3** which reads:

> *Be shepherds over the flock God has entrusted to you. Watch over it as God does: Don't do this because you have to, but because you want to. Don't do it out of greed, but out of a desire to serve. Don't be rulers over the people entrusted to you, but be examples for the flock to follow.* (NOG)

Chapter 18

Transformational

Transformational is another relationship-oriented leadership style. Transformational leadership is defined as a leadership that focuses on motivating the subordinate to go above their personal interests for a shared vision, mission, and purpose. There are four factors involved in transformational leadership style: motivation or inspirational leadership, intellectual stimulation, individualized consideration, and idealized influence or charisma (Giri & Santra, 2010).

A transformational leader is often admired as well as trusted by his followers (Feinberg, Ostroff, & Burke, 2005). Transformational leadership is also future-oriented and focuses most thoughts on what is ahead. When attempting to inspire followers to embrace the vision of the organization, entrepreneurial leaders will find the transformational leadership style most useful. If an entrepreneur is trying to implement organizational change within the business, leaders will find transformational leadership useful as well.

Three years after opening my first business, I was finally ready to open a second location. Realizing that I could not be in two places at one time I decided to hire managers to oversee each location. Each manager was responsible for handling day-to-day business operations and overseeing office personnel. I would travel back and forth between locations daily and bring the managers together for a weekly meeting. I needed to think structure and style to make this arrangement work.

While my managers needed to be able to trust me, I also needed be able to trust them. A leadership style such as transformational leadership was the answer this dilemma, and the business model itself was the deciding factor in my choosing to operate under a decentralized organizational structure. Since I could not always be on location, I had to delegate some authority to my crew. This is yet another lesson for entrepreneurial leaders. The organizational structure and leadership style of choice will depend upon the business model, the goals of the organization, and the task to be accomplished.

God's Instruction

DON'T LOOK OUT ONLY FOR YOUR OWN INTERESTS,

BUT TAKE AN INTEREST IN OTHERS, TOO.

PHILIPPIANS 2:4 (NLT)

As previously mentioned, entrepreneurs are generally transactional leaders. Of course, as an entrepreneur you want to earn money; however, you have to be careful not to ever reach a point where you no longer see your team as people. Don't become so task oriented that you no longer care about the needs of your staff.

Do you know your leadership style?

Rate your leadership now:

Never (N) 1 2 3 4 5 6 7 8 Always (A)

_____ Are you most often motivated by goals and achievements?

_____ Are the personal needs or personal development of your team a primary focus in your business operation?

_____ Do you try to encourage, listen, understand, and address employee needs and wants?

_____ Do you motivate your team to go above their personal interests for a shared vision, mission, and purpose?

What have you gleaned? _____

_____

_____

_____

_____

_____

_____

_____

_____

_____

_____

_____

_____

_____

_____

_____

Part 5

"Diversification and globalization are the keys to the future."

— Fujio Mitarai

Think Globally

The third and final element of entrepreneurial leadership to be discussed is global thinking. Globalization has become commonplace for most business organizations since most of them, inclusive of businesses that are not intending to expand their operations across national borders, take a global context in their operations (Blythe & Zimmerman, 2004). Companies who consider themselves to be strictly local may not even realize that they are in fact global. If organizations have customers across the country, purchase inventory from other countries, or simply use the technology created internationally, then their business is a part of the global market.

Wherever a business's main operations are based, organizations need to adopt a global perspective in their dealings so as to be successful (Edwards, 2011). Several new ventures are increasingly appreciating the fact most new business opportunities are transnational or that new services or products can be developed in distant locations (Isenberg, 2008). For some entrepreneurs, globalization is at the base of their initial business model, while for other business owners, the route to globalization has come out of necessity or evolution. Whatever the path used, your global venture must be led properly. For this reason, when thinking globally, entrepreneurial leaders should take the time to create a global business strategy.

To create a global business strategy, there are two vital actions: (1) globalize your business strategy and (2) globalize your leadership strategy. To globalize your

business strategy, you should create global vision and values, build a global roadmap, and execute your global strategy (Rosen, 2001). Entrepreneurial leaders can create global vision and values through promoting global discussions that express the organization's overall goal; leaders with a global perspective globalize their values as well as their vision (Rosen, 2001). Secondly, entrepreneurial leaders must build a global roadmap. The global roadmap should be structured to guide followers through the stages of globalization.

Lastly, entrepreneurial leaders must create a global enterprise strategy. To accomplish this task, entrepreneurial leaders should create global leadership competencies and develop globally literate management teams (Rosen, 2001). For this reason, experts affirm that developing a course of action for competing in the global market should be a concern of every entrepreneur (ibid.).

The internet, social media, and video communication have successfully removed all national borders, allowing small business owners the opportunity to do business anywhere in the world. Despite being headquartered locally, a global operation on some level is just about a requirement for any company to be successful in today's business climate (Edwards, 2011). As a result, the entrepreneurial leader has gained access to an unlimited number of customers. However, as a result of globalization not only must the entrepreneurial leader be concerned with the competitor down the street but must also look out for the competitor on the other side of the world. Global thinking can help entrepreneurial

leaders to prepare a strategy for how they will compete and succeed in this global economy.

Today, many new ventures are coming to realize that new business opportunities are extending well past the borders of this country and that globalization can actually help them to expand into new business opportunities (Isenberg, 2008). For some entrepreneurs, globalization is at the base of their initial business model, while for other business owners the route to globalization has come out of necessity or evolution. Whatever the path used, your global venture must be led properly. For this reason, when thinking globally entrepreneurial leaders should take the time to create a global business strategy.

Chapter 19

Global Leadership Strategy

Once the business strategy is globalized, the next step is to globalize your leadership strategy. Entrepreneurial leaders can globalize their leadership strategy by improving upon their global competence. To improve upon global competence, leaders should acquire three fundamental traits: inquisitiveness, business savvy, and cultural literacy. Entrepreneurs are better equipped to seek out useful and timely data and to sort through and make sense of that data through inquisitiveness. Inquisitiveness enables leaders to embrace the constant dualities of doing business internationally (Black, Morrison, & Gregersen, 1999).

The next trait is global business savvy. Only leaders that possess global business know-how are in a position to identify global business opportunities fit for their organizations (ibid.). It is crucial that entrepreneurial leaders have the necessary business know-how in a global marketplace, given that globalization also amplifies challenges in addition to availing greater opportunities for the business (Gregersen, Morrison, & Black, 1998). Moreover, a leader who is business savvy sees the world as a borderless market where the "'the sun never sets," as an opportunity for value creation, as opposed to a mere home for humankind (Morrison & Gregersen, 1999).

Finally, entrepreneurial leaders must be culturally literate. Leaders who are culturally literate transcend their cultural background to create business solutions.

They are able to expand their skills and ideas through exploring skills, resources, and markets in different parts of the world (Rosen, Digh, Singer, & Philips, 2000). In reference to global leadership, diversity motivates the success of global leaders. The desire to experience and see new things, as well as their zeal for adventure, compels them to succeed (Gregersen, Morrison, & Black, 1998). Global business often requires an entrepreneurial leader to do business in a country where the leader may not understand the culture or language. Therefore, if the entrepreneur wants to succeed, the leader must have a broader set of skills, skills that qualify them to think and act globally (Edwards, 2001).

When developing a business plan, most entrepreneurs tend to include neighboring communities. The may extend out there reach 25–50 miles. Doing business beyond that radius, most are unable to envision. Initially, I too fell into this category; however, necessity forced me to extend my reach far beyond my surrounding community. As a result, I decided to incorporate the internet into my marketing plan. This allowed me to extend my reach outside traditional boundaries and to offer my services to a much broader consumer base. Companies who insist on remaining strictly local miss out on a world of opportunities and run the risk of business failure. If entrepreneurs are to lead their companies successfully, thinking globally must be included in the overall business strategy.

God's Instruction

ENLARGE THE PLACE OF YOUR TENT, AND LET THE

CURTAINS OF YOUR HABITATIONS BE STRETCHED OUT;

DO NOT HOLD BACK; LENGTHEN YOUR CORDS AND

STRENGTHEN YOUR STAKES. ISAIAH 54:2 (ESV)

Entrepreneurial leaders cannot afford to focus on one area. Globalization provides countless business opportunities and must be considered by all serious business leaders.

Can your company benefit from globalization?

Rate your leadership now:

Never (N) 1 2 3 4 5 6 7 8 Always (A)

_____ Do you exhibit the ability to see and understand the world from others' cultural perspectives?

_____ Do you tend to take a non-judgmental stance towards the ways things are done in other cultures?

_____ Do you have the ability to acknowledge differences in communication and interaction styles?

_____ Are you curious about other cultures, values, beliefs, and communication patterns?

_____ Are you comfortable in communication with foreign nationals?

What have you gleaned? _____

_____

_____

_____

_____

_____

_____

_____

_____

_____

_____

_____

_____

_____

Final Thoughts

The number of new business start-ups and new hires are growing. If the owners of these start-ups are to succeed, effective leadership is a must. An entrepreneur is the captain of their ship. As the captain, the entrepreneur must learn how to develop and improve their leadership skills. To accomplish this task, entrepreneurial leaders should aim to exhibit trustworthy leadership by remaining authentic, having integrity and strong values, and by inspiring those they lead. As written in **Titus 2:7**:

> *Always set an example by doing good things. When you teach, be an example of moral purity and dignity. (NOG)*

As an entrepreneurial leader there is a responsibility to exemplify the behaviors you wish to see in your employees. You can essentially destroy your own business by being less than trustworthy. Entrepreneurial leaders must be able to not only define the vision and moral culture of their company but they must be able to translate the vision into action. To reiterate, leaders should remember the three main factors of leadership necessary for entrepreneurial leadership success: strategic thinking, structure and style, and global thinking.

References

Ashkenas, R. (1999). *Creating the Boundaryless Organization. Business Horizons*, p. 5.

Balkin, A. (1990). What is creativity? What is it not? Music Educators Journal, 76(9), 29.

Bassett, L. (2010). *Unemployed Entrepreneurs: In The Absence of Jobs, Some People Create Their Own.* Retrieved from http://www.huffingtonpost.com/2010/10/21/unemployed-entrepreneurs-_n_771367.html

Black, D. (2013). The Importance of Rest. Retrieved from http://danblackonleadership.info/archives/2652

Black, J. S., Morrison, A., & Gregersen, H. (1999). Global Explorers: The next generation of leaders. New York: Routledge.

Blythe, J., & Zimmerman, A. S. (2004). Business-to-business Marketing Management: A Global Perspective. Cengage Learning EMEA Higher Education.

Bonn, I. (2005). Improving strategic thinking: a multilevel approach. Leadership & Organization Development Journal, 26(5), 336-354. Retrieved from EBSCOhost.

Briner, B. & Pritchard, R. (2008). The Leadership Lessons of Jesus. Nashville, TN: B&H Publishing Group.

Calarco, A., & Gurvis, J. (2006). Flexible flyers: A leader's framework for developing adaptability. *Leadership in Action, 25*(6), 14-16.

Carbone, L. (1996). Integrity, courage, vision: The marks of a leader. *Nation's Restaurant News*, p. 28. Retrieved from Business Source Complete database.

Carland, J. C., & Carland Jr., J. W. (2012). A MODEL OF SHARED ENTREPRENEURIAL LEADERSHIP. Academy Of Entrepreneurship Journal, 18(2), 71-81.

Casey, A. (2010). Enhancing the ability to think strategically: A learning model. Management Learning, 41(2), 167-185. Retrieved from EBSCOhost.

Collins, J. C., & Porras, J. I. (1998). Building Your Company's Vision. Harvard Business Press. p. 339

Daft, R. L. (2007). Organization theory and design. Mason, OH: South-Western Cengage Learning. p. 90.

Darling, J., Keefe, M., & Ross, J. (2007). Entrepreneurial Leadership Strategies and Values: Keys to Operational Excellence. Journal of Small Business & Entrepreneurship, 20(1), 41.

Davis, S., & Lawrence, P. (1978). Problems of matrix organizations. Harvard Business Review, 56(3), 131-142. Retrieved from Business Source Alumni Edition database. p. 134.

Dickson, M. W., Smith, D., Grojean, M. W., & Ehrhart, M. (2001). An organizational climate regarding ethics: the outcome of leader values and the practices that reflect them. Leadership Quarterly, 12(2), 197.

Dunkelberg, W. C. (1995). Presidential address: Small business and the U.S. Economy. Business Economics, (30)1, p. 13, 6p, 4 Graphs.

Dwivedi, R. (2006). Visionary Leadership: A Survey of Literature and Case Study of Dr. A.P.J. Abdul Kalam at DRDL. *Vision* (09722629), 10(3), 11-21. Retrieved from Business Source Complete database.

Dwyer, D. (2007). Lead by Example. *Professional Remodeler*, 11(8), 17. Retrieved from Business Source Alumni Edition database.

Edwards, Sandi (2011). Today's Leaders Should Be Global. Business Source Alumni Edition, 10(3),   54-56.

Ellis, C. (2004). Leaders Who Inspire Commitment. Retrieved from http://sloanreview.mit.edu/article/leaders-who-inspire-commitment/

Feinberg, B. J., Ostroff, C., & Burke, W. W. (2005). The Role of Within-Group Agreement in Understanding Transformational Leadership. Journal of Occupational and Organizational Psychology, 78, 471-488.

Fraher, A., (2010). The Pros and Cons of Decentralized Leadership. Retrieved from http://views.washingtonpost.com/leadership/panelists/2010/09/the-pros-and-cons-of-decentralized-leadership.html

Gallup's Leadership Research – Strengths Homepage. (n.d.). Retrieved from http://strengths.gallup.com/110251/Gallups-Leadership-Research.aspx

George, B. (2007). Authentic Leaders. *Leadership Excellence*, 24(9), 16-17. Retrieved from Business Source Complete database.

George, B., Sims, P., McLean, A., & Mayer, D. (2007). Discovering Your Authentic Leadership. *Harvard Business Review*, 85(2), 129-138. Retrieved from Business Source Complete database.

Gatto, R. P. (1992). Teamwork through Flexible Leadership: A How to Guide for Conducting Business in a Changing Work Environment. Pittsburg, PA: GTA Press.

Giri, V., & Santra, T. (2010). Effects of Job Experience, Career Stage, and Hierarchy on Leadership Style.

Singapore Management Review, 32(1), 85. Retrieved from Business Source Alumni Edition database.

Gray, J. H., & Densten, I. L. (2007). How Leaders Woo Followers in the Romance of Leadership. Applied Psychology: An International Review, 56(4), 558-581.

Hatch, M. J., & Cunliffe, A. L. (2006). Organization theory, 2nd ed. New York, NY: Oxford University Press, Inc.

Isenberg, D. J. (2008). The Global Entrepreneur. *Harvard Business Review*, 86(12), 107-111.

Jones, R. A., Jimmieson, N. L., & Griffiths, A. (2005). The Impact of Organizational Culture and Reshaping Capabilities on Change Implementation Success: The Mediating Role of Readiness for Change. Journal of Management Studies, 42(2), 361-386.

Kippenberger, T. (2002). Leadership Express, Capstone Publishing, Inc., p. 7.

Klein, K. E. (2006). Dousing the Flames of Burnout. BusinessWeek Online, p.4

Kouzes, J. M., & Posner, B. Z. (2007). The leadership challenge (4th Ed.). San Francisco, CA: Jossey-Bass.

Kouzes, J. M., & Posner, B. Z. (2008). The Five Practices of Exemplary Leadership. San Francisco, CA: Jossey-Bass.

Kuratko, D. F. (2007). Entrepreneurial Leadership in the 21st Century. Journal of Leadership & Organizational Studies (Baker College), 13(4), 1-11.

Lambert, E., Hogan, N., & Allen, R. (2006). Correlates of correctional officer job stress: The impact of organizational structure. *American Journal of Criminal Justice*, 30(2), 227-246. Retrieved from EBSCO*host*.

Maitland, A. (2010). What about "the rest"? *Conference Board Review*, 47(4), 68-69.

Majumdar, S. (2008). Modeling Growth Strategy in Small Entrepreneurial Business Organizations. *The Journal of Entrepreneurship*, 17(2), 157-168. Retrieved from EBSCO*host*.

Mancheno-Smoak, L., Endres, G., Polak, R., & Athanasaw, Y. (2009). The Individual Cultural Values and Job Satisfaction of the Transformational Leader. *Organization Development Journal*, 27(3), 9-21. Retrieved from Business Source Complete database.

Milazzo, V. (2012). Emotional Energy. *Personal Excellence, 17*(9), 9.

Miller, C. (1995). The Empowered Leader: 10 Keys to Servant Leadership. Nashville, TN: B & H Publishing Group.

MindTools.com (1995-2010). *Leadership styles.* Retrieved November 3, 2010 from http://www.mindtools.com/pages/article/newLDR_84.htm

Moyer, D. (2006). Best with a Rest. *Harvard Business Review, 84*(3), 152.

Nordmeyer, B. (2013). Centralized and Decentralized Organizational Structure. Retrieved from http://yourbusiness.azcentral.com/centralized-decentralized-organizational-structure-3785.html

Northouse, P. (2007). Leadership: Theory & Practice. Thousand Oaks, CA: Sage Publications, Inc.

Putting Creativity on the Company Agenda. (2011). Industry Week/IW, 260(3), 12-14.

Quong, T., & Walker, A. (2010). Seven Principles of Strategic Leadership. *International Studies in Educational Administration (Commonwealth Council for Educational Administration & Management (CCEAM))*, 38(1), 22-34. Retrieved from EBSCO*host*.

Rakov, C. (2001). Why Values-Based Leadership Will Help Your Company Outperform Its Competitors. Retrieved from http://www.metaforceagents.com/pdfs/Why%20Values-Based%20Leadership.pdf

Saloner, G. (2011). Innovation: A Leadership Essential. Bized, 10(1), 26-30.

Sanders, T. I. (1998). Strategic thinking and the new science: Planning in the midst of chaos, complexity, and change. New York: Simon & Schuster.

Shelton, C. (2010). Trust-Powered Leadership. *Leadership Excellence, 27*(4), 20. Retrieved from Business Source Alumni Edition database.

Stanley, A. (1999). Visioneering. Sisters, Oregon: Multnomah Publishers, Inc.

Surie, G., & Ashley, A. (2008). Integrating Pragmatism and Ethics in Entrepreneurial Leadership for Sustainable Value Creation. Journal of Business Ethics, 81(1), 235-246. doi: 10.1007/s10551-007-9491-4

Teasley III, C., & Ready, R. (1981). Human Service Matrix: Managerial Problems and Prospects. Public Administration Review, 41(2), 261-267. Retrieved from Business Source Alumni Edition database. p. 261.

Thoms, P. (2004). Driven By Time: Time Orientation and Leadership. Prae.

Wager, M. (2011). Inspire your team. New Zealand Management, 58(10), 64.

Transport Industries Benefit from Innovative Thinking; Innovation is no less important during an economic downturn than it is when business is booming and there are resources to spare for creative-thinking. (2009). M2PressWIRE.

Wager, M. (2012). How to become an inspirational leader. *NZ Business, 26*(3), 46.

Weiner, B. (2009). A theory of organizational readiness for change. *Implementation Science, 4*(1), 67. Retrieved from E-Journals database.

Wing, M. F. (1997). Are you a strategic thinker? Management Review, 86(8), 62. Retrieved from EBSCOhost.

About the Author

A gifted visionary, Dr. Juanita Fletcher has been commended for her innate ability to look past the problems of today straight into the possibilities of tomorrow. With over thirty years of leadership, entrepreneur, and business management experience, Dr. Juanita Fletcher has become a skilled teacher and mentor. In addition to teaching, Dr. Juanita Fletcher is also experienced in strategic planning, organizational design, and change implementation. Driven by a strong sense of urgency and incredible resilience, she thrives on massive change in crisis situations. Dr. Juanita Fletcher is at the top of her game when turning uncertainty and chaos into order and harmony.

As an entrepreneur Dr. Juanita Fletcher launched

Available Insurance Agency in 1997, which she then sold to Nationwide Insurance in 2002. In 2011, Dr. Juanita Fletcher launched GHME Productions, Inc., a full service production company complete with recording, photography, and videography services. Since the company's introduction, it has added three subsidiary companies: Glitz, Hair, Music & Excitement (2011), ACHI Magazine (2013), and ACHI Magazine Awards Gala (2014). Today, Dr. Juanita Fletcher oversees day-to-day operations as the Chief Executive Officer.

Dr. Juanita Fletcher holds a Doctorate of Strategic Leadership from Regent University, a Master of Management and Leadership from Liberty University, a Master of Divinity from Virginia Union University a B.A. in Christian Leadership from Tidewater Bible College and an A.A. in Ministry from Tidewater Bible College. In

addition to her business aspirations, Dr. Juanita Fletcher is a national gospel recording artist with three recorded projects to her credit, and with the completion of this book she can now add 'author' to her resume.

Dr. Juanita Fletcher is available for speaking, teaching and vocal engagements. To book Dr. Fletcher contact:

GHME Productions, Inc.
1226 Executive Blvd., Suite 103
Chesapeake, VA 23320
(855) 829-7225
www.juanitafletcher.com

www.ingramcontent.com/pod-product-compliance
Lightning Source LLC
Chambersburg PA
CBHW020206200326
41521CB00005BA/266